Table of Contents

Golf For Beginners

How To Improve Your Technique And Swing Like A Pro!

Terry McMillman

Introduction

Famous author Mark Twain once wrote, “Golf is a good walk wasted.” Many people feel this way. After all, what’s so fun and interesting about hitting a little white ball with a metal stick trying to get it in a little hole? However, the truth is there is fun to be had on the golf course as is evidenced by the millions of golf enthusiasts all over the world.

Ever since the game of golf was invented back in the 15 th century, people

have been fascinated with mastering this often frustrating game. In 1750, the game of golf evolved into what we know it as today, and since that time, technology and technique has improved on the game, but mastering the game of golf still lies in the individual playing the game.

One of the great things about golf is that it is more than a physical sport. Your mental state can play a huge part in your golf game. If you hit a bad shot, it can really affect your next stroke and so on and so forth. It's important to realize that if golf were less challenging, it wouldn't be nearly as much fun.

People can spend thousands of dollars in efforts to improve their golf game. They buy videos, books, new equipment, and lessons from a professional. Improving the golf game is a multi-million dollar industry as it seems like there are all sorts of people offering advice on things you can change to improve your score.

Just as the golf swing has been improved upon over time, so has the equipment used to play golf. In the 1800's, golf bags came into use as an easier way to carry around clubs and balls. Golf balls were made lighter and able to travel further and tees were used to help make the ball easier to hit off the tee box.

But even with all this new technology, no one has really perfected the game of golf. If that were the case, there would be scores of 18 with a hole in one on every hole. The truth is that even the professionals can't perfect their golf game. Man is fallible and he makes mistakes. But when it comes to the game of golf, mistakes are inevitable.

I've heard many golfers tell me that they played great but scored horribly. That statement made me really think about my own golf game. I, too, have had rounds where I've hit the ball well but it wasn't reflected in my score. How is it possible that we can hit the ball so well yet still take a 6 on a par 4 hole? The answer isn't easy, but it can be addressed.

I'm not a golf pro, but I do love the game of golf. I've always wanted to improve my golf game, so this book will help both you and me. I decided that researching what the pros have to say would be a great way to put their advice to good use. Compiling all of that information into this book would also be a great way to share that advice.

Let's look at different aspects of the game of golf and find some easy ways to improve our scores!

Equipment Needed

Believe it or not, the equipment you use in your golf game can truly make a difference in how well you strike the ball.

With new technologies in club designs and materials used to make the clubs, you can get overwhelmed at the various choices you will have when buying golf equipment.

We'll look at this section from the perspective of your skill level.

Beginner – Average scores over 100

Because you are just learning the game, you will want to have clubs that are more forgiving when you make bad shots – and those bad shots will come. The beginning golfer should be looking for clubs that are the most forgiving when the ball is struck off-center. Perimeter-weighted clubs place the most weight of the club around the edges, which prevents the club head from turning with a poorly hit shot.

If you would like something that makes it very easy to get the ball in the air, you should look for irons that have more sole weighting. Sole weighting lowers the center of gravity by putting the weight under the ball, helping to get it in the air quicker.

Titanium is stronger, denser and lighter than steel, thus the club head can be made larger with the same amount of material. A larger head also means the size of the sweet spot will be larger. Since off-center shots will make you lose distance, a larger sweet spot will be the most forgiving.

Some heads feature an "offset" design to prevent your shots spinning left-to- right and giving a straighter ball flight. The offset means the face is slightly behind the hostel of the club head. This gives you an extra split second in the swing to get the face back to the square position.

For your driver, the larger the head the more forgiving it will be. These are all going to have the largest face, producing the largest sweet spot. This is very important, since a beginner doesn't always hit the ball right in the middle of the clubface. (Studies have shown you lose 10 yards for every 1/8" of an inch you miss the sweet spot!!!)

For fairway woods, the lower profile woods make it easier to get the ball airborne, as the weight is mostly below the center of the ball.

Graphite shafts are the most forgiving shafts for poorly hit shots. They absorb the vibration like a shock absorber, allowing for a much better feeling shot. Graphite shafts are lighter weight, so you will pick up some swing speed which will give you more distance.

For this reason graphite shafts are more popular than steel shafts in the metal woods when distance is your primary goal.

Steel shafts don't feel as soft, and they are heavier, but they are more accurate than graphite. For this reason, they are usually better for the irons, since you are less concerned with distance and more concerned with accuracy since you are hitting into greens and at the pin.

Intermediate – Average scores between 80 and 100

The intermediate golfer should be looking for a club that maximizes both distance and control. The more perimeter-weighting you have, the more forgiving the club, but the more weight directly behind the ball gives you more distance. These club heads all seek to optimize the balance between distance and control.

You should look for distance clubs with titanium heads. They are very light, allowing you to generate more club head speed to get more distance, yet still more controllable than the largest of the oversize titanium heads.

For intermediate golfers, any shaft would work well. It's important that you pick out the properties of a shaft that will help your game the most. The lightweight shafts have a lower flex point, which help you get the ball in the air quicker.

The standard weight shafts have a higher flex point, which allows for better control. Graphite shafts and the True Temper Sensicore shafts have a bit softer feel.

Advanced – Average score less than 80

Advanced golfers need the weight of the club head where it is needed most... right behind the ball. The weight is more directly behind the ball, meaning a shot struck in the center of the club will explode off the club face.

The advanced golfer will want a driver with a large head so the sweet spot is larger and you have a better possibility of longer drives. Irons should be lightweight with the proper degree of loft for all situations.

If you are an advanced golfer, you probably already know what clubs work best for you and where you need to upgrade.

Test out various clubs and find which ones are good fits for you. Practice, if possible, with different styles and take note of those that give you the best results.

When it comes to golf balls, you will want those that can give you the most distance and that aren't too "hard". There are many brands on the market that can fit into this mold, so test out a few and see which one you like the best.

So you've got your equipment, now let's take a look at some of the basics of golf and a good, effective golf swing.

The Basics Of Golf

The purpose of this book isn't to teach you how to swing a golf club. However, it can never hurt to go over the basics of the golf swing and the golf stance. So often, we get into bad habits on the golf course when it comes to our swings. We forget the things we initially learned about and start swinging the club in really the wrong way.

Everyone has their own golf swing style. Very few people stand the

same way, have the same backswing, and hit the ball the same way. For that matter, very few people are able to duplicate a swing exactly the same every single time. But there are some basics to a good golf swing that everyone should keep in mind.

The full golf swing is an unnatural, highly complex motion and notoriously difficult to learn. It is not uncommon for beginners to spend several months practicing the very basics before playing their first ball on a course. It is usually very difficult to acquire a stable and successful swing without professional instruction and even highly skilled golfers may continue to take golf lessons for many years.

So let's just go over the basics of the golf swing first – just as a review.

The Grip

There are three basic golf grips that you can use: the overlapping

grip, the baseball grip, and the interlocking grip. We'll cover each of those in a minute. Here's the basic rule for gripping a golf club.

Start by holding the club directly in front of you with your right hand with the club head pointing away from you at about a 45 degree angle.

Next grip the club with your left hand. The club will be mainly in the palm across the pads at the base of the fingers. However, the club will lie across the first section of the index finger. The thumb will be positioned straight on top of the golf club shaft. Relative to the golf club, the thumb will be in the twelve o'clock position.

Now, with your right hand, grip the golf club just above your left hand with the fingers, not the palm, of your right hand. The thumb will be

positioned slightly off to the left. Relative to the golf club, the thumb will be in an eleven o'clock position.

If you have gripped the golf club correctly, only the first two knuckles of your left hand will be visible. Also, your left thumb should be completely hidden under your right hand. The index finger position of your right hand will look and feel like a gun trigger finger.

Here are three of the most common golf grips and how to use them:

- The overlapping grip is the most common golf grip used. It is used mostly by male golfers and those with strong wrists and forearms. The little finger of the right hand lies on top of or overlaps the index finger on the left hand.

- The baseball grip is most commonly used by younger golfers, females, seniors, and those with weaker wrists and arms. The index finger of the left hand and the little finger of the right hand meet but do not overlap or interlock.

- An interlocking grip will be used by golfers with shorter hands and fingers, those with thicker or chunkier palms, and golfers who have difficulty with the overlapping grip. The index finger of the left hand and the little finger of the right hand overlap each other and interlock.

If your golf grip pressure is right, the club could almost be pulled out of your hands, but not quite. A correct golf grip will make you feel as if you are holding the club mostly in the palm and last three fingers of your left hand. Regardless, both hands should hold the club with equal pressure. A correct golf grip doesn't guarantee a successful golf swing; however, a defective golf grip will almost always result in a failed golf swing.

Your Stance

If you start with a bad golf stance, you'll probably follow with a bad golf back swing, a bad downswing, and a bad follow through. Not to worry though. It's just not that difficult! Your golf stance may not be perfect, but you can compensate by staying balanced and relaxed. Your weight should be equally distributed over your left and right leg. If you can pick either of your feet off the ground, you're not balanced.

Start by placing the inside of your front foot just ahead of the ball. Since you're going to be using a driver or 3 wood, the front and back feet should be shoulder width or slightly more than shoulder width apart.

Next, bend at the top of the legs (keep your back straight) and then bend slightly at the knees. The kneecaps will be directly above the balls of your feet. The angle of your back to the ground will be approximately 45 degrees. Your arms should be hanging straight down from your shoulders.

Good posture counts. Keep your back straight but don't tense up. You might think of it as pushing your back pockets higher.

Your weight should be on the balls of your feet, not on the toes or heels. Likewise, your weight should be equally distributed between your front and back foot. Now you should be more comfortable and less tense. If you're out of balance, you're falling down. That's no way to start a good golf swing.

A line drawn across the front of your feet should point to your target. You may want to check this by first placing your club up against the toes of your feet and then step back and see if the club is really pointing to your target. This is your target line and your knees, hips, and shoulders should also be parallel to this line.

One slight adjustment will be the position of your shoulders. When you assume the proper golf stance and grip, your club and left arm will form a straight line between your shoulder and the ball. For this to happen, your right shoulder will be slightly lower to the ground than the left, but a line through your shoulders should still be parallel to the target line.

Once you grip the club and take your stance at the ball, find a way to relax and loosen up before you start your swing. You may want to waggle – or shake your tush - just a little bit and to heck with those who might laugh at you. Once you hit that monster shot, they'll stop. Now you're ready to swing.

The Backswing

Essentially, the backswing is a rotation to the right, consisting of a

shifting of the player's body weight to the right side, a turning of the pelvis and shoulders, lifting of the arms and flexing of the elbows and wrists. At the end of the backswing the hands are above the right shoulder, with the club pointing more or less in the intended direction of ball flight.

The downswing is roughly a backswing reversed. After the ball is hit, the follow-through stage consists of a continued rotation to the left. At the end of the swing, the weight has shifted almost entirely to the left foot, the body is fully turned to the left and the hands are above the left shoulder with the club hanging down over the players' back.

Instead of thinking about your arms and swinging your club

backwards, try to think of your back swing as turning your back to the target. You're not swinging the club up in the air; instead you're just putting the club behind your back. It's like winding a spring!

The back swing works from the top down. The back swing takeaway starts at the top with your arms and shoulder turning, and it works its way down to your hips and legs.

The back swing is all about coiling up your body and creating the muscle tension or torque needed to release a powerful downswing. More specifically, resistance is created between the greater turning of the upper body and shoulders and the lesser turning of the hips and lower body.

Don't get in a hurry! A hurried back swing doesn't make the

downswing any faster. In fact, it may be just the opposite. You've got to remember that somewhere at the top of that back swing, you've got to change and go the exact opposite direction.

The speed of your back swing should be at a steady tempo, not real fast or real slow. The tendency is to go too fast. Any time your golf swing begins to break down; your first correction should usually be to slow down my back swing.

Turn your back toward the target or, maybe better, think of turning your chest away from the target. Pick the thought that produces the greater feeling of coiling or resistance. Don't allow the back knee to fly outwards. Keep your weight towards the inside of that foot.

Your wrists should be completely cocked by the time your left arm is parallel to the ground. The golf club shaft should be at a 90 degree angle to your left arm.

Don't focus on the club head during the backswing. Instead think of the arm as being hinged at the left shoulder. Then, like a gate that swings open from its hinges, the left arm hinges at the left shoulder and swings across the body until it approaches the right side at my right armpit. The left arm remains relatively straight, but could bend slightly.

Your shoulder and upper body turn begin as the left arm reaches this

position. As the arms go back, two things should happen:

1. The forearms will naturally rotate clockwise slightly until the golf club head points to the sky. Opening the club face more won't seem right to you

if you tend to slice, but don't resist this very natural movement.

2. As your arms travel up and back and the golf club shaft approaches parallel to the ground, you will gradually begin cocking your wrists. Then by the time that your left arm is parallel to the ground, your wrists should be completely cocked at a 90 degree angle.

Cocking your wrists is a very important part of creating club head

speed. This is often a big swing problem. You can get so concerned about "taking the club straight back" at the beginning of your back swing that you

don't completely cock your wrists. Fixing this problem can straighten out several golf swing problems.

The next part of the golf swing is the shoulder and upper body turn. The left arm has swung across the body near the right armpit. The natural continuation of this motion is to begin the turning of the shoulders. The shoulders will turn from parallel to the target line to approximately perpendicular to the target line depending on your own flexibility. As this happens, the hips and then legs will also become involved in the turn.

Wouldn't you like to feel more body torque build up in your golf back swing? Of course! A friend gave me this golf swing tip just the other day. Maybe you'll find it to be as helpful as I did.

Instead of trying to create body torque by turning your shoulders, think of turning your lower chest (Let's say about six inches above your bellybutton) away from the target. Of course when you do it this way your shoulders will still turn but you should feel much more torque building through your body.

Don't let the knee of your back leg turn or fly out or to the back as the

back swing progresses. You'll lose part of your body torque.

At the height of the back swing, you'll feel like your back is over top of your back leg. At this point your weight has shifted back over your back leg.

It is truly a myth that the head stays over the ball as at address and the body turns on an axis formed by a line traveling through the head and the backbone. In reality, the body turns on an axis formed by a line traveling through the head and the back leg. Keep in mind that the head is moving slightly backwards. The head should stay fairly level and not bob up and down.

Where are the arms and club at the end of the back swing? Should the golf club be parallel to the ground? Honestly, you shouldn't really don't give that much thought. As long as you don't bend the left arm more than slightly, these positions will be determined by how far you can turn your upper body.

If you keep your back knee in, the back foot will feel your body

weight on the inside as the shoulders turn. Towards the end of the golf back swing, some golfers make the mistake of letting the heel of their front foot leave the ground. If the back swing coils the spring, the feet must stay anchored to the ground to give the body something to coil against. Better to let the front foot roll or sort of lay down on the inside of the foot without dragging.

If you start with a correct golf stance, grip, and back swing, the best advice for your down swing for the most part is to just let it happen!

The down swing and follow through should be the very natural result of everything that precedes it.

You may want to use the “No Arms Drill” in the next section to memorize the feel of the golf swing which leads to a more comfortable, automatic golf swing.

If you’re at the correct position at the top of your back swing, your body will start to unwind releasing the golf club which will strike the golf ball and lead to a balanced follow through.

Think of the follow-through as your victory salute to a successful golf swing! Your front leg will be fairly straight and your hips will be forward forming a straight line with your front leg.

Your head may feel like its back a bit and your back leg will be

forward of the back foot which has rolled to the inside, front of the foot. Most all of your weight will be on your front foot, completing your weight shift from the back side to the front side.

This is like a barometer of your entire swing. When your golf swing is balanced and smooth, you end with that nice reverse C position at the end.

On the other hand, you could end your golf swing off balance and catching yourself from falling down. Then it's time to go back to the beginning of your golf swing and find where you lost that balance.

You should have only one swing thought during your golf down

swing. That's because you really don't have time for two. Consequently, your only thought should be to turn your belt buckle (or bellybutton) towards the target as fast as you possibly can.

This movement should begin about a third or half way through the golf down swing. It will end, of course, when you are pointed towards the target at which point you will have already hit the golf ball and you're into the follow through. And you should also be seeing the golf ball traveling straight down the fairway!

On the golf down swing your body will move forward and turn on an axis formed by a line traveling through the head and the front leg. Keep in mind that the head will be moving forward from its position at the end of your golf back swing; however, the head should stay fairly level and not bob up and down.

Since the golf down swing starts from the bottom and works its way up, then the feet are the place to start. Let's see, at the end of the back swing, the front foot was rolling (almost laying down) on the inside of that foot.

Consequently, a good trigger motion would start by moving the left

side towards the target and placing that foot back to being flat on the ground.

To trigger this move, you should plant your front foot by moving the front knee towards the target. Your lower body will slide towards the target.

Since both knees are still slightly bent and flexed, this move will give you sort of a squatty look and feel. You might feel as if you're dropping down slightly. Planting that front foot begins the chain reaction of your body uncoiling and your weight will shift back to the left (front) side.

What you do not want to do is start the down swing with your arms

and shoulders. This move will cause your wrists to un-cock too soon (called casting) resulting in some pretty nasty results (topped shots, slices).

The most effective golf swing tip I've found to prevent casting is also a very logical one. Begin your down swing before you finish your back swing. Makes sense! You're not likely to start your down swing with your arms and upper body if they're still winding up.

So, as you feel your upper body approaching the end of the back swing you will move your front knee towards the target. As you do this, you'll feel that low, squatty position and know that you're starting your back swing properly with the lower body.

Often the golf swing feels uncomfortable and awkward, so you may want to try the following drill until you start feeling better about the golf swing.

No Arms Drill

Remember, I said you should probably be spending less time thinking about what your arms are doing and where they're going? Once my wrists are cocked, I really don't think much about my arms.

This golf swing drill, simply put, is just practicing your golf swing without using a golf club. Consequently, you'll be able to concentrate on the feeling of your muscles coiling up and releasing without being confused or distracted by the movement of your arms.

This is also a good opportunity to practice keeping your feet on the ground. Practice having your front foot roll inward on the golf back swing and memorize that feeling.

Another upside to this drill is that you can practice it anywhere or

anytime.

Begin by getting into your regular golf stance. You can place a ball

down in front of you or imagine where it would be if that helps. Now instead of holding a golf club, cross your arms in front of you to where your left hand is at your right shoulder and your right hand is at your left shoulder.

Try not to do this drill fast or slow, but at a steady tempo. Do this drill frequently and memorize the movements and how they feel so you can do them without think when you're on the golf course.

Again, the golf back swing starts at the top (your shoulders and arms) and works its way down to your hips and legs. Remember, your head will move to the back but should not bob up or down. It should stay level.

Of course, in this drill you don't use your arms, so you begin by turning your shoulders. I find it more beneficial to think of turning your midsection (Let's say about six inches above your bellybutton.) away from the target. Of course when you do it this way your shoulders will also turn. Get comfortable as you are feeling the torque building through your body.

As your shoulders and hips turn, remember to not let your right (back) knee turn outwards (towards the back). This will have the feeling of pushing that knee inwards and/or keeping your body weight more on the inside of the back foot.

Feel the front knee turn inwards and the front foot rolls towards the inside but still stay on the ground.

Start from the bottom. This golf swing drill is a good time to practice moving your front knee towards the target as a trigger to your down swing. Don’t forget to start that move before the back swing is complete. Get comfortable with that low, squatty feeling.

Turn your hips with the swing thought of turning your belt buckle to

the target. You will feel like your hips are leading the rest of your body. The shoulders will follow as you pivot on your front leg.

Use this drill to commit to memory, or muscle memory, any movement that isn't a swing thought.

In a slight variation of this drill, you could start the golf back swing with your arms (no club).

Practice hinging your arms at the shoulder and cocking your wrists as your arms cross your chest near the back arm pit triggering your shoulder turn.

And that's the basics of the golf swing. You won't get any better unless you practice, but if you have good solid mechanics in your golf swing, you have the beginning to a great game!

We've already said that golf is much more than just a physical game. It's a mental game as well. You have to keep a positive mindset when on the golf course, so getting your mind in the right place is very important.

Your Mental Game

When you begin to address the golf ball and prepare for your swing, it's essential that you have a sense of relaxation. If you are tense when you swing your club, the chances of you hitting a bad shot are increased by leaps and bounds. However, you don't want to be TOO relaxed lest your grip isn't tight enough to hit the ball solidly.

Without relaxation, it is more difficult to maintain your tempo or

rhythm from swing to swing and stay in good balance from start to finish. Because it is essential for the golf swing to function properly, relaxation of the mind and body should be our first priority. Please keep in mind that this also applies to the short game, even though I will be referring to the full swing.

Tension restricts movement. A quiet, relaxed mind and body allows you to swing more freely. Simply stated, muscle groups respond more easily to a natural, balanced swing motion.

If your mind is tense, your muscles will be too. If you have had a

hectic day at work or at home, chances are you will take that tension and anxiety to the first tee. This tension not only causes tight muscles, but can also increase the speed of your swing.

When that happens, the little muscles (hands and arms) take over the big muscles (shoulders, hips, and legs) throughout the golf swing. The big muscle groups cannot move as fast as the little muscles. All body parts must be given time to do their jobs efficiently and in harmony.

First, clear your mind. Picture your mind as a blackboard, and written on it are all the thoughts and happenings of the day. The key is that you've got the eraser! Erase your mind of everything and take a moment to put yourself in an environment that makes you relaxed, quiet and happy.

Envision yourself listening to soft music, reading a good book,

relaxing in your favorite chair, strolling in the park, hiking, fishing, walking on the beach, or simply being in the mountains.

Basically, pick whatever image that helps you relax, and then put your mind and senses in that personal place. Be explicit. Actually hear the music or the waves. Feel the warm breeze or the water flowing around your body. See the mountains in all their glory. Smell the flowers. Take a deep breath and let it out slowly. Allow your mind and body to come down so that you can be up and ready to play a good round of golf. Now your mind and body can focus more clearly on one shot, one hole at a time.

Second, practice more relaxation in your grip, stance, and swing.

Check the tension level in your grip. The hand pressure on the club should be light. If it is too tight, your takeaway will tend to be jerky and too fast. If you are not sure of the amount of pressure, let your hands feel the difference by squeezing tightly and then releasing to a very light grip.

Notice that when you squeeze tightly, your forearms are tense. This generates tension throughout the body. You want just enough grip pressure so that you won't lose the club during the swing. No white knuckle! What little pressure you do feel should be in the last three fingers of the let hand, and the third and fourth fingers of the right.

When addressing the ball, your arms should hand relaxed. The forearms should be soft - like ashes, wet noodles, or any other descriptive word of your choice that triggers relaxation. If your left arm is jammed straight, tension is created in the shoulders. I've seen some golfers who looked like they were trying to jab their left shoulders into their left ears.

The left arm should hang comfortably straight and the shoulders should droop. The legs should also be set in a relaxed starting position. Trying to force your weight to your insteps can cause lower body immobility.

Now waggle! The waggle helps keep the body loose and in motion. Freezing over the ball can cause tension. Chances are you are thinking too much, and paralysis of analysis can set in. Develop a waggle that is comfortable to you.

Most waggles consist of moving the club to and fro over the ball (not up and down) with a slight weight shift back and forth from foot to foot, while you look at the ball, then to the target, then back to the ball.

If you do not have a clear picture of what a waggle is, observe golfers on television or other golfers on your course. Waggles vary, but good golfers always stay in motion.

Most importantly, your waggle must be one that you are comfortable with. Each person has his or her own waggle personality. Find yours and practice until it becomes ingrained in your swing routine. You can work on this in your backyard.

Initiate the swing and swing relaxed. To practice a relaxed swing, take continuous swings back and forth without stopping. Be aware of any tension you might feel during these swings. Try to stay totally relaxed and loose as you swing back and forth. Don't be in a hurry to start or finish the swing. When you get to the finish, allow your body to be lazy in returning the club to another backswing. No jerks!

Notice whether your hands and forearms tense when initiating the first swing of the series. If they are tense, then repeatedly practice starting your swing with a feathery grip pressure so that no tension runs through to your forearms and thereby to the rest of your body.

Tension can cause quite an array of problems such as reverse pivots;

fast takeaways; forced swings; loss of club head speed; rolling on the outside of the right foot; incorrect swing plane; fat or topped shots; big and little muscle groups not working together; lack of balance; or a fast tempo that your swing cannot handle with any efficiency.

A major problem with even professional golfers is that it is so easy to let our minds take a wide sweeping view of what the next shot means:

"How will it affect my score?"

"What does it mean to me personally?"

"Is this the best round I have ever played? Is it the worse round?"

"If I sink this putt it will put me one up on my opponent!" "My dad is watching, I really want to do well."

All of these comments, questions and statements are possible, along

with hundreds more, at the very time you need to be focused on the elements of planning and executing the shot. If you are doing this, you are not "boxing out" the shot.

"Boxing out" means that you mentally put up a fence around what you need to do, so that you are not distracted by the things and thoughts that have no real bearing on the shot or putt. By not "boxing out" you allow your mind to wander to distractions.

Remember: even pleasant thoughts of success are not relevant to making the shot. Sometimes this lack of limiting your thoughts is called "outcome thinking". In other words, you spend time and energy thinking of what the outcome could be and how that would feel. This is truly an unwise way of spending the time and energy needed to make the shot.

Think of a piece of paper with words and pictures covering it. All of

these words and pictures are in some way related to the next shot, but only a few of them are helpful in making the shot. Now group the needed and useful elements together on the page. Now draw a box around these few things.

Some of the things in the box would be: a solid plan to make the shot, a solid pre-shot routine, feeling the swing or putt in your mind, seeing the ball go to where you want it, and ending up looking at the back of the ball as you swing or putt.

Things left out of the box are: past mistakes, thoughts of how bad it would be to miss the target, thoughts of how good it would be to make the shot, or just about anything else you could think of. All of these are left out of the box because they do not help you make the shot.

It is important to really understand what should be in the box. Make a list of what is important to making the shot. You may even what to consider the sequence or order of the included thoughts. Any other thought or picture is out of the box and not allowed. If you find anything in the box that does not belong in there, simply pick it up by its tail and drop it outside the box. Practice limiting your thinking to only what is in the box.

Begin by practicing at home. Practice "boxing out" fifty times at home before you begin to practice it in physical practice. After two or three weeks of practice you will be ready to begin to use this in competition. Remember, you must first practice mental training at home and then in physical practice before you can expect to use it in competition.

One of the most effective changes that a golfer can bring into his or her game is called step-breathing. The benefits of using step-breathing are many. You give yourself a solid, focused mental and physical place from which to hit your shots or make even the longer putts, you have a time to find the best level of mental arousal, and you gain more control over your playing tempo.

Another advantage of taking the time and centering yourself with step- breathing is that it places a nice dividing line between the thinking part of your golf swing and the hitting part. The old saying is; "The thinking must stop before the hitting begins."

You begin to learn step-breathing at home. You simply sit in a comfortable chair and imagine a side view of a set of stairs. When each stair drops down, this is your exhale. When the stair is flat, and horizontal to the ground, this is your inhale.

In normal breathing your breath in and out and really never move

lower in your body. If you were to graph a normal breath it would be a "U" shaped curve. It would go down on your exhale and back up on you inhale. Your breathing would be one long line of "U" shaped curves. This is fine for taking in oxygen, but not very effective for centering your mind and body to maximize your golf.

You continue your training by practicing lowering your center of

breathing from high in your chest, near your throat, down to your lowest point in your stomach. Following your six or seven steps down into your body, remember the exhales are when you drop a little further down and the inhales are the flat part of the step. On the inhale you do not go down, but you also do not go up, as in a normal breath.

Once the breathing is very low in your body practice keeping it there for four or five breaths. Then let it gradually come back up. If you practice this exercise one hundred to one hundred and fifty times you will begin to find that the breathing begins to anticipate your lowered center of breathing and your breathing will automatically drop on the second or third breath.

When this happens you have learned the ability of using the short form of step-breathing. The short form of step-breathing utilizes this learned reaction and allows you to become fully centered using only two or three breaths. On the course, or even in practice, you will need to use this short form of step-breathing so that you can quickly get centered and ready to take the swing or the putt.

After you have learned the short form of step-breathing you are ready to make it part of your pre-shot routine. After you have planned your shot, addressed the ball, recalled a successful shot like the one you are about to make, you can use the step-breathing to end your thinking, relax your body, lock your expectation on the exact target and be externally focused on the ball. No thinking, no worrying, no wobbling of focus and fully ready to put the ball where you want it.

Now that you can center your breathing, begin to use it on the practice tee. Practice your pre-shot routine before each shot. (Did you think the practice tee was only for physical practice? How will you find your best game if you only practice the physical aspects of your game?

Establish your exact target, complete the step-breathing short form,

focus on the ball and let yourself hit the ball. By practicing the entire routine you will soon be very comfortable with the procedure and your scores will reflect your new level of mental and physical control.

Do not try to utilize this or any other mental training technique until you have understood the theory and concepts involved and practiced the mental technique to the extent that you are able to fully use the procedure. Then bring it into competition after you have used it in practice several times. There are no short cuts to improving your game. You need to do the work and do it in the right order before you can really enjoy the higher level of play it brings.

Start practicing your long form of step-breathing today and soon you will have the mental control you need to play your best game.

After a mild winter many golfers are ready to hit the links with

renewed vigor. Unfortunately, high hopes will be dashed quickly if you can't keep your emotions in check. Here's an example of how we like to have 'Pity" parties for ourselves when we aren't playing too well.

There was this guy in west Texas delivering a package to a house out in the rural countryside. He pulls up and sees an older gentleman on the porch in his rocking chair. A few feet away there was a dog-moaning and whining away. "Excuse me, Sir." said the concerned delivery guy to the older man on the porch. "What's the matter with the dog?"

The old man, with an attitude of indifference replied. "Oh, he's layin' on a nail."

The delivery man asks "Why in the world is he doing that? Why doesn't he just get up?"

The old man shrugs his shoulders and says, "I reckon he ain't hurting bad enough yet!"

Well I think we have all met people like that pitiful dog-spending time whining and complaining about how their golf game is so bad and why they can't play well. Instead of complaining about how life is treating them unfairly they won't take the initiative to do something about their situation and change their circumstances. Sometimes people like to take umbrage in their miserable plight and they enjoy company whenever possible.

Nothing is going to change until you start hurting bad enough to do something about it. This of course applies not only to your golf game, but life in general. In fact, if people spent as much time looking for the solutions to their golfing problems as they do complaining and making excuses most of their problems would scurry away like that frightened dog.

Instead, they throw a "pity party" and are put out when no one shows up to attend. Life is too short to waste time and energy on such negative thoughts so move on and get some help for your game.

So "get off layin' on the nail." and you can start having success and fun on the course again. "Break that old broken record" that has you playing that same sad song and taken your game into tailspin. There's a great old saying that goes," If you always do what you've always done. You'll always get what you've always got." It's time to start seeing the 'Light through that dark tunnel' you have built for yourself.

Mark Twain once said, "You can't depend on your eyes when your imagination is out of focus." There is a multitude of reasons why we bury our games into submission and none of them are good. It's time for you to start believing and seeing yourself pulling off the shots you dreamed about instead of worrying about where disaster is lurking ready to strike you down on the course and ruin your round.

Many players say that even when they're playing good they are

anticipating the proverbial wheels to come off at any moment. I read a statistic somewhere that 92% of what we worry about or fear never comes to fruition: meaning that you’re wasting your time on meaningless things distracting you from your goals.

Stop concerning yourself with past events or things in your game that you have no control. "You can't water yesterday's crops with today's tears." Let it go and move onward!

It's a good practice to mentally play a round in your mind where you control the ball and place it where you want it to go avoiding all the problems such as water, out of bounds, sand, etc. Try it sometime and let your imagination run wild.

Take notice of this mental exercise to see if you allow bad thoughts to enter your mind even in your pretend round. Bad habits die hard and the first place to attack them is in your conscious mind.

In order to eliminate bad habits that you have formed in your game try this 3 step process:

1. First confront your fears in your game and admit them by writing

them down on a piece of paper.

2. Replace it-it's time to trade in bad habits and negative behavior for good ones.

3. Stick with it-by being persistent, diligent and remaining disciplined your game plan you'll be soon forming a new habit.

We can't change our circumstances about how the ball bounces so to speak, but we can alter our response to them. It's all about choice so choose wisely. Having a brighter outlook about playing and excepting occasional bad breaks that are inevitable will help you start getting over being "Teed off" about yourself and your golf game

However, sometimes losing your cool can be good because it can help you let off some steam and help you refocus on the task at hand. Often, as all golfers know we keep it bottled up which can impair our performances for the rest of the round.

The key is to allow yourself to completely vent, then refocus again immediately. By venting I don't mean throwing or breaking clubs, or cursing. The skill of refocusing lies in knowing what the most important element to master is. How does a person learn to regain composure after losing it?

Just remember that losing your cool is nothing more than focusing on what went wrong, and allowing yourself to get frustrated, angry, ticked off, etc. Think about how you respond when you’re angry - you breathe faster, your body tightens up, your heart rate increases and so on.

These stress messages you’re sending to your brain only make your body tighten up more sabotaging your abilities to perform properly. This unfortunate cycle will continue until you learn to break this broken record set on self-destruct.

In a tense situation the best way to regain your composure is to work in the opposite direction, to get your body to calm down, this in turn will allow your mind to calm down by taking several deep breathes, and by pushing away any negative thoughts.

There's a good method called "Treeing" which seems appropriate since you're on the golf course with plenty of trees. What you do is take your emotions in this case negative thoughts and put them onto something else.

Some older cultures throughout the world have used this technique for centuries. They learned to pass their bad feelings or negative emotions to a tree, hence the name. So next time when you're on the golf course and you're losing your cool find a tree and push or touch it physically releasing your pressure that you're feeling into the object and leave it there.

After you have dealt with the past it's time to move on to the future which in this case is a new hole, or shot at hand. Remember you can't change the past, but you can profoundly affect your future with the proper mind set. There's no longer a reason to carry all this emotional baggage to the next hole so let it go. So next time you see a player in the woods a lot during a round maybe they're just getting rid of some issues that are bothering them.

This is all easier said than done, but like all things with a little practice and some discipline you'll be recovering from poor shots quicker and

salvaging your round instead of going from bad to worse. The best players in the world all have their own particular methods for staying cool, so watch how they handle poor shots while they are in town.

It's traits like staying cool when everyone else is losing their heads that make the difference from being a good player to becoming a great player.

So many people are harder on themselves than they need to be.

Constantly berating yourself is a recipe for disaster. The dialog that you hold with yourself is critical to your development as a player and as a person.

Self-talk can be encouraging or it can be detrimental, according to how you present it to yourself. Remember: Your mind doesn't have a sense of humor. If you program it to do something and the message is negative, it will respond accordingly.

This is why it's important to monitor your inner dialog; what you say to yourself after a poor shot can be self-destructive. Even the best players in the world are guilty of this mistake, and if they don't make corrections immediately, the round or tournament is lost.

We've all beaten ourselves up after a bad day on the links, or when things don't go our way. If you watch a tournament on television,

periodically you'll see a player bad-mouthing themselves. They might be saying things such as, "I'm the worst golfer in the world," or "Why can't I hit that simple putt? I stink." These statements or other expletives will bring the golfer down.

The key is to change how you talk to yourself while practicing or on the course. I've taught and worked with a number of sports psychologists over the years who gave me some good insight about how to break negative self-talk patterns.

First, you need to be aware of situations when negative thoughts can occur.

Here's a simple method to get you started on the right track: The next time you head out to play a round of golf, put a handful of pennies in your right pants pocket. Not too many to weigh you down, though.

Every time - and I mean every time - you become aware of negative images or internal dialog where you're speaking poorly to yourself, transfer one penny from your right pocket to your left pocket. By learning to monitor your thoughts, you're on the right path to correcting your inner demons.

When you're finished playing, count out the number of pennies that made the journey from one pants pocket to the other. Then write down the total. Try to remember what words you used, and what situations prompted them.

Then, start setting some new, clearer goals. In this case, the goal is to attempt to cut down on the number of negative self-talk speeches. Just like you have goals to shoot certain scores, you need to apply this same attitude with correcting this debilitating self-talk.

Once you have been able to calmly re-examine your round and your

outbursts of negativity, imagine yourself reacting to those circumstances in a different way and replacing those negative statements with positive thoughts. Learn to laugh with yourself and say, "I can do this shot," and other such positive feedback to reinforce your self-worth.

With each round, make a conscious choice to reduce the negativity and try to remain positive - remember it's only a game. With some diligent practice and commitment, you're on your way to erasing bad thoughts about your golf game.

Now that we’ve covered what should be going on in your head, let’s take a moment to examine each of the most important golf shots.

Golf Shots & Techniques

DRIVING THE BALL

While driving the golf ball might seem like a simple process, it really isn't. Some seasoned golfers just look at driving the ball as a simple process. "Grip it and rip it" is a common phrase you can hear on many tee boxes. However, there are some things you can do to get more distance on your drives.

First and foremost, you need to be relaxed when you begin addressing the ball. You must be loose before pulling back the club. Do not tighten up over the golf ball. It is important to waggle the club back and forth a few times in order to create some flow to start the golf swing. This action will promote proper rhythm and tempo.

Teeing the ball higher will aid in hitting the ball farther. By teeing the ball higher, it will help achieve better launch angle and reduce backspin at impact. This will allow the ball to be hit on the up-swing - producing more carry and distance.

One of the most valuable pieces of advice this recreational golfer ever received was to look at the back of the ball. It's easy to take your gaze off of that little white orb, but if you are not looking at the ball before you hit it, you will be more likely to miss it.

You will want to have a wider stance in order to gain more stability in your backswing. Approximately sixty percent of your body weight on the left side to gain a more powerful coil. If you're right handed, point your left toe more inline to the target. You'll need to swing harder and put more of your right hand into hitting the ball, and take advantage of all of the elements – especially the wind, if there is any.

When you're at the top of your backswing, be sure to turn your shoulders a full 90 degrees. Your back should actually be facing the target. Look at John Daly when he drives the golf ball. He has a massive shoulder turn. Many players ask him all the time how he does it. He says it's due to having a sound technique and a wide swing arc. He always has a rhythm to his golf swing and is never out of sync on his swing.

After you reach the top of your backswing, you're ready to begin the downswing. Do not rush your downswing. If you do, you'll have an increased chance of swinging straight down on the ball and eliminating any power you had going. You will also most likely chili dip and miss hit the golf ball. Look at Fred Couples and his downswing. It's nearly flawless.

Make sure to keep your left arm straight during your transition. When you keep your arm straight it enables the club head to remain square and hit the ball properly. Don't have a herky-jerky swing. Keep your golf swing smooth. Picture yourself hitting through the ball, not just to it. Hit hard with your right hand.

Be sure to take advantage of the playing elements to help give you

more distance; especially using the wind to your advantage. When you have the wind at your back, you should tee the golf ball higher than normal. This gives you a higher ball flight with more carry in the air. That means greater distance. When you're playing into the wind you want the opposite. Tee the ball down a little more than usual.

As mentioned before, you will want to look at the ball before hitting it. Some players find this difficult as it makes them lose focus as they concentrate too much on the ball. An easy answer to this problem is to turn your chin to the right and point it about two or three inches behind the ball. Keep it there until impact and then watch the ball sail through the air.

Believe it or not, the pressure you use to grip the club is important in

driving the ball longer. Even though you may think that gripping harder and swinging harder produces results that is absolutely incorrect and is probably why you don't get consistent distance.

The great players indicated that the grip pressure should resemble one holding a bird without crushing it but also not letting it go. The tighter you hold the club, the less it will release through the ball creating severe pulls and big ballooning slices. Swinging hard is ok but the hands must be tension free.

Your driving wood should stay along the ground for a least the first 20 to 25 percent of your swing. If your club is lifting up, you will pop the ball up and not get that long boring drive that you see the pros hit regularly when the ball takes off like a missile and slowly climbs to a beautiful height and tracks down the fairway.

Keep the angle on your leading hand. Many amateurs tend to flip the hands forward in an effort to get the ball in the air, but this only retards the effort of having good equipment. The leading hand (left hand for most players, right hand southpaws) should be angled down towards the ball on the downswing.

It's like you are hitting the ball with the back of left hand. If your left hand is flipping up on the downswing, your contact will not be solid and you will get consistent misses with your wood. This tip also starts the ball low and lets its climb on its own through your generated power.

Finish towards the target. Pick a spot on the ground that lines up with your target and from your address stretch your wood towards it. If done correctly, your arms should form a V shape with both arms fully extended. Finish the swing over your left shoulder.

Do you have a tendency to bend your left arm early? That also will

retard distance; keep your V as long as possible before it bends at the finish of your swing and you will find yourself getting much more distance.

Speed can be increased by setting the wrists into a cocked position early, and on the downswing keeping the wrists cocked for as late as possible, and then swishing through the ball. This is similar to flicking your wrists when using a badminton, squash, or tennis racket.

Golfers who are inclined to hit at the ball with their hands rather than swinging through the ball find that they lose a lot of power, and hence distance. Your power comes from your body, not from your hands. If you want to drive the ball further, don't hit the ball with your hands – let the club do the work it was designed to do.

Of course, you will want to choose the right club for the distance of

the hole. Obviously, you will want to choose a driver for the longer holes to get maximum distance, but for shorter holes like Par 3s, you will likely want to choose a smaller club like an iron. You will want to try and get as close to the hole as possible, but you also don't want to overshoot the green either.

The best way to know how far you can hit specific clubs is to get on the driving range. Because golf isn't an exact science, there are a lot of variables that come into play with the golf swing. But if you practice a lot, your chances of hitting the ball consistently are much higher. Plus, you will know which club is your hundred yard club and which one is your 50 yard club.

After you have driven the ball, you'll (hopefully) be in the fairway.

FAIRWAY SHOTS

Once you have driven off the tee box, you will probably be faced with a second shot, hopefully from the fairway. Of course, we hope that you've been able to make it to the green, but on longer par 5 holes, that's just not realistic for most golfers.

The lie of the ball in a fairway shot will dictate how you hit your next shot. In some friendly games, your opponents may allow you to put the ball up on some grass. This will emulate, in a way, a tee since you cannot use a tee with a fairway shot. In tournaments or serious money games, you will probably have to play the ball as it lies, so it's a good idea to know how to hit an effective fairway shot.

Many inexperienced golfers are intimidated by the fairway shot. They will often baby their swing and not hit the ball fully. This is a huge mistake. Golf clubs are designed to work with a full golf swing and do a specific job, so choose a club that matches your distance from the hole and then take a full swing. Don't be afraid that you'll overshoot the hole. If you've picked the right club, you'll get to the green.

Aim your left shoulder (the right one if you're a southpaw) at your target – the flag. Your hands should be in front of the ball at impact. Keep the same swing motions as if you are driving the ball. To help square your clubface, try to touch your left forearm with your right forearm at impact.

If you are in deep grass, the main idea is to get the ball up in the air.

That means you will want a club that has a lot of loft. That means an 8 or 9 iron ideally. However, remember that you will most likely not get a lot of distance with these smaller clubs.

When you swing, be sure and follow through after impact. The laws

of physics dictate that when you strike the ball, it will be carried through and into the air as your arms bring the club back up.

Your technique on deep grass shots should be geared toward

minimizing the intervention of the grass. In other words, you want to hit the ball as cleanly as possible. To do that, you need to move the ball back in your stance.

If, for instance, on a 5-iron shot from the fairway you position the ball off your left heel, move it back to a spot an inch to the right of your heel for a shot from the rough. This ball position should leave your hands slightly ahead of the clubface at address. From that setup you'll tend to swing the club up a bit more vertically on the backswing and return it a bit more steeply to the ball. With this steeper attack the clubface will come down on the ball rather than brush through the grass.

For really deep grass, again, the idea is to minimize the presence of

the grass and how it will affect your shot. Once again, play the ball back in your stance, but this time, play it two inches back instead of one, because you're going to have to go down after the ball.

To further increase the steepness of the swing, open your stance a few degrees so that your feet, knees, hips and shoulders align to the left. Your club head should align square to the target line. It's the same basic alignment as for a slice, but when playing a short iron from the rough 1 you won't have to worry about any sideward spin.

Since the grass will grab at your club and close the face: at impact, you'll want an extra-firm grip in your left hand. Alternatively, you can aim the clubface a bit right of your target at address, thereby allowing the grass to turn the face into a square position at impact.

The swing should be an aggressive, forceful one. If you get a kick out of swinging hard, this is the place to enjoy yourself. It's a powerful, steep chop that must go down and through the thick stuff. Be sure to keep the club accelerating through impact; otherwise you'll risk moving the ball only a few feet. The faster you can get the club moving through the ball, the faster that ball will climb out of its nest and the farther it will go.

Eventually, you’ll be close enough to chip.

CHIPPING

This is the part of golf that many golfers have the most trouble with. Because chipping requires a bit of finesse, it’s much easier to flub a shot or overshoot the hole. There are some good techniques you can use when chipping the ball up onto the green.

There are two parts to a successful short game: the plan and the

execution. The plan is simply defining your shot before you play it. You should determine where you plan to land the ball and how far it will roll. The plan should include landing the ball on the green whenever possible and playing the best percentage shot. The best percentage shot is usually the one that is simplest to execute.

Since you are hitting the ball a shorter distance than with a full swing, you should choke up on the club, narrow your stance, and stand closer to the ball. Picture the shot you're about to play and make a practice swing to approximate the swing you'll need. The club should be swung with arms and shoulders, with some wrist break. The key to shots around the green is to "keep the arms moving".

As with other golf shots, picking the right club is essential to an

effective chip. First of all, chip shots are essentially those played from right off the green. Most are otherwise known as "bump and runs." Don't confuse them with pitches, which are lofted shots with a sand-wedge.

Many of us have been taught over the years to get the ball on the green as soon as possible and let it roll to the hole. There is nothing wrong with this. This is fine.

The issue of concern, however, is when golfers go about playing different length of chips with an assortment of clubs. They hit a 9-iron if the flag is 20 feet away, 8-iron thirty feet, 7-iron forty feet, etc. You should really just choose ONE club to hit all of your "bump and runs" with, and adjust for the distance with the force of your swing.

It can be a 5, 6, 7, 8, 9, wedge, or sand wedge. It doesn't matter that much. A great player, Phil Mickelson, likes to use his sand wedge in just about every case. He will play it far back in his stance, with his hands way ahead to bump it. On the other hand, Corey Pavin often uses a 5-iron around the green. He just "taps" it and the ball goes scurrying across the green with a lot of topspin.

These are extremes, however. You should pick a 7, 8, or 9-iron. I,

personally, like to use a 9-iron for chipping. I know how the ball is going to come off of the club because that's the one I practice with all the time. I have tried using a 7-iron on longer chips, but the ball seems to explode off the club face because I am not sure the proper force that I need to use.

The art of chipping is hard enough without having to master four or five clubs. Practice with a couple at first. You should hit short "bump and runs" from the fringe and then longer "bump and runs" from in front of the green.

From there, decide which one you like better, which one you can

control the spin better with, and ultimately which one that you can control the distance better with. Then, put the other one in the bag, and practice with the one you chose. Master this one club approach and your chipping will improve dramatically.

You will want most of your weight to be focused on your lead foot. For right handers, that would be the left foot. Your swing should be in a pendulum motion with no wrist action. If you break your wrists on a chip shot, your ball is going to shoot to one side or you may overshoot the hole altogether.

As we've said, you often won't want to take a full swing when chipping. Gauge the distance you are away from the hole and then estimate how hard you'll have to hit the ball to get it to the hole – or at least close to the hole!

Here are some general tips on chipping that can really help:

Keep your hands ahead of, or even with, the club head on the follow- through.

Grip the club firmly so that the rough doesn't twist the club on the swing.

Get the ball rolling on the green as soon as possible; this will make it easier to control the shot

In deep rough, angle the club so the toe is the only part touching the ground.

In windy or downhill conditions, or on fast greens, always chip the ball instead of pitching it.

Repair all divots taken.

Be careful not to hit the ball too hard; otherwise it might roll off the other side of the green.

Chipping should not be confused with pitching. When you chip a ball, you are going to be just off the green and you want the ball to easily roll across the green and toward your target. A pitch shot is a lofted shot that flies more than it rolls. A pitch is usually used when you are a little further off the green but you still are close enough that you won't want to take a full golf swing.

A pitch shot is usually from 30-70 yards away from the green. You can also use a pitch shot if you need to hit above trees, hazards, or sand traps.

Use a lofted wedge club like a sand wedge, a pitching wedge, or a lob wedge. These clubs have faces that allow you to get underneath the ball and put it in the air.

You will want an open stance with your feet closer together. The ball should be positioned in the center of the stance. Your body turn will be determined by the size of the swing. Focus about 70 percent of your weight on your lead foot.

You will have to modify your backswing according to the distance you have to go to the hole. It can be waist high, shoulder high, or a full swing. Just don't put too much power into it or you will overshoot the green. Let your legs and body turn slightly through the shot.

As with any shot, your aim should be to present the clubface perfectly square to the target. But this is even more important with the pitch, as any minor deviations will be magnified by such an intense shot. Aim for a ball then turf contact. If you are regularly thinning the ball when attempting this shot, you are probably not accelerating into it.

Once on the green, you'll want to putt effectively. There's nothing more frustrating than taking more putts than what you need to.

PUTTING

Again, many golfers have trouble with their putting. I know of one experienced golfer who can consistently drive the ball 250 to 300 yards only to get on the green and three putt. Nothing frustrates him more, but putting is an important part of your golf game – possibly THE most important part.

Stroking the ball is only one part of putting. To putt effectively, you first need to know how to read a green. That means looking at the trajectory your ball will travel and compensate for any dips, hills, or anything else that could cause your ball to move a specific way.

Good green reading comes with experience. After hitting enough putts over enough different types of terrain and grass, you develop a sixth sense of how the ball will roll. As you walk onto a green, whether you realize it or not, you take in all sorts of subtle information.

If the green appears light, you know you're putting against the grain; if it's dark you're down grain. If the green is set on a high area of the course and you feel a breeze as you step onto it, you sense that the putt will be fast. Even if you don't look closely at the surrounding terrain, you are aware of any major slope in the land.

Without having to tell yourself, you know which the low side of the green is and which the high is. If the putting surface is hard and crusty under foot, you receive one message; if it's soft and spongy you get another. Experience with many, many putts allows you to run this data through your computer before you even mark your ball.

The most elusive aspect of green reading has to do with the grain. Grain refers to the direction in which the blades of grass grow. The light/dark appearance is one way to read it. Another method you can use is to take your putter blade and scrape it across a patch of fringe. If the blades

of grass brush up, you're scraping against the grain. If they mat down, you're scraping with it. (Incidentally, be sure to do this scraping on the fringe. On the greens, it's against Rule 35-1f.)

A third method is to take a look at the cup. Often, the blades of grass will grow over the edge of the cup in the direction in which the grain moves. Incidentally, grain usually grows toward water, especially toward the ocean, and in the East it's apt to lean toward the mountains. If you're not near any such topography, figure on the grain growing in the direction of the setting sun.

Grain is strongest on Bermuda grass, where short, crew-cut-like blades tend to push the ball strongly. Although each putt on each green is different, as a general rule you can figure on stroking the ball about 20 percent harder than usual on a putt that's dead into the grain, and about 20 percent less on a down grain putt.

When the ball breaks with the grain, you need to read-in extra

"borrow" on the putt. When the slope is against the grain, play for less break. These effects are less marked on the long-stemmed bent and other strains of grass, but they are present nonetheless.

The break of your putt will also be affected by the firmness of a green, the wetness/dryness, the amount of wind you're facing, and even the time of day. In general, any time you have to hit the ball hard, you play for less break.

Another way of reading the break on a green is to watch the way other players' putts behave. I'm all for this "going to school," but with one caveat:

Allow for any difference between your own playing style and those of your fellow players. If, for instance, your friend is a lagger and you're a charger, don't play as much break as he does.

Finally, one hard and fast rule in putting is this: Never hit the ball until you have a good vision of the path on which it will roll. Sometimes the vision will come to you immediately. You'll see the perfect putt the minute you step up to it, and more often than not, you'll sink it just as you saw it.

Other times, it will take much longer to get a picture of the putt, and even then you won't be comfortable. But don't make your stroke until you have the best read you can get. You have to believe in your line if you want to have a good chance of sinking any putt.

If the green is located near water, you can bet the ball is going to

break towards that body of water. I'm not sure why this is, but it is certainly true.

It's essential that you know you shouldn't be aiming for the hole.

Good putters know that you have to pick a spot on the green and then aim for that spot. For example, if you think the ball will break three inches to the right, pick a spot three inches to the left and shoot at that spot.

Don't think of a putt as a curved shot – think of every putt as being

straight on. When you have your spot, aim to have the ball travel right over that spot. If you have read the green correctly, the ball will naturally travel into the hole.

Don't rush reading a green. Take a look at how your ball lies from all angles. Walk around it; look at it from across the pin to see the trajectory that the ball needs to travel at. But have respect for your fellow golfers. Don't take forever reading a green. It's not rocket science and you won't want to hold up play.

Keep in mind that the line of the putt has little to do with being able to put the ball in the hole. Good putting depends on the speed of the ball when it leaves your putter's face. But achieving that speed can be quite elusive. There's no easy way to judge how hard you need to hit the ball to get good speed. However, there is something you can do.

Go to the practice putting green. Hit several putts with about a 12- inch backswing. Do this over and over until you can get a good idea of how far the ball will go with that 12-inch backswing. Then when you get on the real green, you can use that putt as a reference to determine how much you will have to add or take away from your backswing to sink the putt.

The way you grip your putter can make a difference in accurate putting as well. You can choose what's best for you, but most professional golfers know that gripping a driver and gripping a putter should be two different animals.

You will want complete control of your putter for the most accuracy. One technique that can help you do this is to modify your grip so that both of your index fingers are extending down either side of the shaft and your thumbs are placed together on the top of the shaft. This can help you guide your putter smoothly and improve your accuracy.

When in your stance, you need to be positioned directly over the ball. I like to call this hovering the putt because you are hovering over the ball like a mother hovers over her children. Set the putter square to the target and have the ball positioned right in the middle of the club face – which most people refer to as the "sweet spot".

Keep your body free of tension and your body motion limited. When you swing, you should do so in a pendulum-like motion using your shoulders not your hips. Always follow through with your putt and accelerate through the ball. Your follow through should be about the same distance as your pull back motion and you need to keep your eyes on the ball at all times.

And most golfers know that if you are faced with either an uphill putt or a downhill put, you should always go with the uphill choice. A downhill putt is much more complicated because of gravity whereas when you putt uphill, you can gain more control of your stroke.

Good putting is essential to a good golf game, so practice as much as you can and try to be consistent in all you do.

SAND TRAPS

Ah, those fairway bunkers – the golfer's bane. Sand traps are a reality on many courses, and you will probably find yourself having to shoot out of them on a fairly regular basis. Although we certainly hope that's not the case, it certainly is possible. Knowing how to effectively hit out of a sand trap is another huge part of a good golf game.

First, don't be afraid of the bunker shot. Sure, it can be intimidating, but you can develop good technique that will get you out of the sand and back on the grass – even on the green.

Establish firm footing and take an open stance. Open the clubface by turning it to the outside before hitting the ball. This will put loft on the ball and allow the back portion of the bottom of the club to bounce off the sand instead of having the leading edge dig into the sand. You will want to use a wedge for this shot – preferably a sand wedge.

Distribute most of your weight to the left side of your body. You will swing the club back and through the same distance. Don't let the clubface close and accelerate through the ball. Don't let the club touch the sand (a big rules no-no) and concentrate on hitting the sand about two inches behind the ball.

What you are trying to do is take as little sand as possible without making contact with the ball. You want the sand to life the ball out of the bunker. As you make contact with the sand there should be a cupping of the left wrist.

Let me explain "cupping." Assume you are wearing a watch on your left wrist and the face, as usual, is pointing outward. When contacting the sand on the forward swing, you should try to take the back of your left hand and move it towards your watch face, thereby creating wrinkles underneath your left wrist.

This action is called "cupping of the wrist" and it is very necessary in producing quality sand shots. Since this motion prevents the club from closing, the ball is lifted in the air with backspin.

You will want to have a neutral grip on the club. You don't want to use a strong grip for bunker shots because it's absolutely essential that the club face slides under the ball and into your finish without the club face closing.

A neutral grip is one that has the back of the left hand facing parallel to the target line and the right palm facing the same direction. Slap your hands together in front of you and you'll instantly see what I mean. You can also choke down on the club in an effort to gain more control.

Aim the club face down the target line which should be just left of the hole. You've heard all the hype about opening the club face and such and that's fine if you hit a lot of bunker shots but most folks don't so aim the club face down the target line which should be just left of the hole. The target should be just left of the hole because this method will impart some left to right spin which will move the ball from left to right once it gets on the ground.

Aim your feet on a 20-30 degree angle to the left of the target line. The greater the angle you create between your feet and the target line, the higher and softer the ball will come out of the trap. Practice these shots a bit with varying angles and you'll see what I mean. Find the angle where you're most comfortable and which produces the best results and stick with it whatever it might be.

This all works for balls that are lying on top of the sand, but what do you do if your ball is buried? The technique is different.

When your ball is buried (fried egg) in the bunker, you do not want to swing super long and follow through. The idea is to pick your sand wedge up abruptly, swing down steep, stick your club in the sand, and leave it there. What will happen is your ball will pop out. It won't have any spin on it because of the lie, but the chance of it getting out of the sand are much better than if you were to follow through.

Why is this so...? You want a very steep angle of attack and no follow through on this shot because it allows for the club to get more underneath the ball. With some of the ball resting below the surface, you need to compensate to get underneath it. That is where a short, steep, punchy type of swing works best.

A typical bunker shot calls for an open stance, an open clubface, and a nice shallow swing while taking a little bit of sand. That will not work with a plugged lie, regardless of how hard you swing. Your club will be approaching from too shallow an angle.

You will hit the sand to the RIGHT of the ball, instead of hitting the sand UNDERNEATH the ball. Thus, your club will just bounce, or deflect into the ball. Worse yet, you will plow too much sand into the back of ball and it will go nowhere. You need to get below the ball somehow.

Here's what I recommend from a buried lie in a greenside bunker:

1. Set up with a bit squarer stance.

2. Square the clubface a bit also. This will allow for the leading edge to

enter the sand first.

3. Pick the club up steeper, and then swing down steeper and stick the

club in the ground. Hit about 1-3 inches behind the ball. You can swing hard, just don't follow through. You won't be able to follow through if you make the correct swing, because you will be coming down too steep. That's good!

This is not a shot that you will face a lot, but I still think it is worth practicing. Go to a practice trap and step on a couple balls to bury them a little. Then hit some shots. Experiment a bit. Especially get the feeling of that up and down "chopping" motion, and that no follow through release. By doing so, you will find that this shot is not really that hard to get out of the bunker.

After a round of golf while socializing in the '19th Hole', you will always hear "I hit the ball well but didn't score." The object of the game of golf is to score the lowest possible score you can. How you can hit the ball well and not score can be summed up in two words: course management.

Course Management

You can ruin a good round by trying to pull off that one in a million shot and making a triple bogey. After hitting a shot into trouble you are almost always better off to take a safe route out and play for a bogey.

What exactly is course management? Essentially, it means adapting your game to the specific nuances of the course and playing the course in the best way you can to achieve a good score.

When does course management start? Some players will tell you it starts after they have to make a decision on the course. Nothing could be further from the truth. Course management starts before you tee off on the first hole. You should always have a plan for the round you are playing and more importantly you should always have a plan and a target for each and every shot.

One particular area that most all golfers should concentrate on is hitting the ball from 125-150 yards out to the green. By improving your game in this area you'll give yourself many more chances for birdie and par putts.

The key to this aspect of your game is being able to "know" that you can hit the ball onto any green from 150 yards out. You want to get to the point where you can consistently knock on 8 or 9 iron onto the green every time!

It may sound difficult if you're a higher handicap golfer, but it's really not. 125 -150 yards is very manageable, and most greens are large in size. In addition, hitting 8 and 9 irons are much easier to control than your longer irons.

If you have a tough time swinging these clubs then this is an area where you need to spend some quality practice time on. Once you do get this down, the only part left is distance management.

That's the first key. The next point is working your game around the 150 yard shot.

If you're on a 550 yard par 5, you know if you hit a decent drive and even if you hit your second shot poorly, leaving you with 135 yards to the green, you know you can now get it on the green with your third shot.

So, even though you didn't hit a great second shot, because you have the 150 yard shot in your bag you're still putting for birdie. This is what good course management is all about.

It's amazing what focusing on this part of your game can do for you. You'll see your golf game differently. Now you'll know that no matter what kind of trouble you get into off the tee box, all you need to do is get your ball 135-150 yards out and you'll be fine.

Practice until you can master this shot. Then build your golf game with that thought in place. By doing so, you won't be worrying as much on how to hit bunker shots, chips shots and other tough greenside shots.

Instead of being completely frustrated, you'll find yourself having more fun.

Once you have this shot in your bag, then you can focus on putting, driving, or hitting your long irons. Until then, put all your efforts into mastering the 125-150 yard shot. If you will take this advice I can honestly tell you that you will dramatically lower your golf scores.

You have to know what your strengths and weaknesses are on the golf course. This is essential to the principles of course management. You must know how far you can hit the ball with specific clubs in order to navigate the course in as few shots as possible.

When you are managing the course, you are taking into account the problems and strengths of your game and applying them to the way the course is laid out. Let's look at two examples:

1. You are on a par 5 hole with light rough on the left side of the fairway and a lateral water hazard up the right. You're pretty confident you can hit the green in regulation, but you have a propensity for hitting a "banana ball" or a hard slice. How should you hit this shot taking into consideration the way you play?

Most players would just hit it up the middle trying to hit the ball straight hoping to keep the water out of play. However, that water hazard is the hole's strength and your slice is your weakness. It's foolish to pit the two against each other because you will probably be the loser.

Aim your teen shot to land in the rough on the left side of the fairway. In this case, your normal slice will result in a second shot from the fairway while a straight ball will result in a second shot from the rough. However, you will probably still be able to reach the green in regulation from the rough.

Most fairways are at least 40 yards wide. If you aim 10 yards to the left of the fairway, it would take a 50 yard slice to get the ball to the water. A shot with that much curve is rare, so this is definitely the best way to play this hole.

2. You are 150 yards from the green with the pin placed at the front of the green, but the pin is tucked behind a menacing sand trap. You've spent a lot of time practicing getting out of the sand and on the green in one shot, but you're not confident enough in your ability to do it just yet. Your 150-yard club is an 8 iron. What do you do to try and avoid landing in the bunker?

Most golfers would automatically reach for their 8 iron, and "take dead aim". However if you were to play with sound course strategy, you would take a 7 iron and aim for the middle back of the green leaving a straight forward two putt for par.

Most people would be afraid of going over the green, but you know that your 7 iron goes a maximum of 165 yards. Even if you hits your best shot you will still have a 45 foot putt for birdie. You also know that if you miss hit the 7 iron it will wind up pin high and in almost no circumstance will the dreaded bunker be in play.

On the other hand if you choose the 8 iron, it will require a near perfect strike to get the ball to the flag. The slightest miss hit results in your ball landing in the sand trap. Here, the 7-iron is the right club based on the layout of the hole.

Putting course management into play with your golf game requires a good working knowledge of the way you play and what you are capable of doing. That means you need to track your progress and really pay attention to how your game is coming along.

Course management skills can really help shave strokes off of your score. So can knowing what the most common mistakes and problems golfers have along with ways to combat them.

Improving Your Game

As we've said numerous times, golf is not an exact science. Many golfers have worked for years and years trying to perfect their swing and improve their game. However, problems do arise. They come about mostly because golfers tend to forget the basic mechanics of the game and start playing sloppy.

In this section, we'll address some of the more common problems golfers have along with mistakes they make. We'll also offer up some suggestions to help you combat these problems and get on the road toward playing better golf.

The Slice

A slice is a specific left-to-right trajectory shape for a golf ball created by a significant tilt of the spin-axis of the golf ball to the right, or a clockwise spin. This is opposite for lefties. A slice usually ends up right of the target line, and the term is often used when the curve in the trajectory is extreme and unintentional. The less extreme version of a slice is called a "fade".

In understanding the basics of the golf swing, in order to hit the ball squarely and straight every time, you must return to the original spot at impact. A slice is caused by the club face being slightly open at the point of impact, thus causing the ball to spin in a clockwise motion, (opposite for lefties). In most cases the swing path is correct, but the golf ball is not being hit squarely at the point of impact, commonly caused by what is known as a "weak grip".

A second factor that causes a golf slice may be swing speed and shaft stiffness. If you use a stiff shaft driver try a regular flex or mid flex shaft and that may correct your problem.

The simplest fix for a slice is in the grip. By having a "weak grip", a grip that is turned more counter-clockwise, (opposite for lefties), can cause the club face to open at the time of impact.

You should start by turning your grip slightly to the right, (left for

lefties), thus giving you a "stronger grip", not holding the club more tightly. Remember the basics and only hold the club tight enough to keep control. You should not have any tension on your wrist and forearms.

You may want to try increasing your swing speed by pulling the club farther back before swinging to fix your golf slice. When you increase your swing speed you can gain yardage and will hit the fairways more often.

Make sure not to bend over too far or round house your swing similar to a baseball swing. Bring your club back straight and follow through on the swing.

Point the label on the ball in the direction you want it to go when

teeing it up. This way you can concentrate on the ball without looking up.

Then, when you tee up your ball, follow this checklist faithfully:

Stand Straighter

Bend Knees Slightly

Keep Feet Shoulder Width Line Up Ball with Front Foot Tip the Club Face in Just a Bit Loosen Your Grip

Keep Your Eye on the Ball Clear Your Mind

Now Hit the Fairway

Draw/Fade

The less extreme version of a Hook is called a "Draw", and the less extreme version of a slice is called a "Fade". Many golfers find that they are only having a draw or fade with their longer clubs, and they are very accurate with their shorter clubs.

Both the draw and the fade are both products of a stronger swing and can be normal. Many golfers use the fade and the draw to their advantage. Slight modifications to your swing will correct both problems, but be careful; tampering with perfection could lead to disaster.

If you are consistent with the fade or the draw, my advice would be to continue to play either shot, just slightly change your aim. If you are inconsistent in your shots and you sometimes fade, draw, slice or hook, look into getting back to the basics and modify your swing to correct your inconsistencies.

Hook

A hook is a specific right-to-left trajectory shape for a golf ball created by a significant tilt of the spin-axis of the golf ball to the left, or a counter-clockwise spin. This is opposite for lefties. A hook usually ends up to the left of the target line, and the term is often used when the curve in the trajectory is extreme and unintentional. The less extreme version of a hook is called a "draw".

In understanding the basics of the golf swing, in order to hit the ball squarely and straight every time, you must return to the original spot at impact. A hook is caused by the club face being slightly closed at the point of impact, thus causing the ball to spin in a counter-clockwise motion, (opposite for lefties). In most cases the swing path is correct, but the golf ball is not being hit squarely at the point of impact, commonly caused by what is known as a "strong grip".

As in the slice, the hook is often a product of an improper grip. Start by looking at your current grip. Remembering the basics of the golf grip, you should only see 2 knuckles of your left hand. If you see 3 knuckles, then you have a "strong grip" and this maybe the cause of your golf hook.

You can fix your hook by trying to change your grip to a "weak grip". Turn your hands slightly counter-clockwise on your grip, (opposite for lefties), thus weakening the grip. Grip pressure is also a key element in the release process. If the pressure is too loose at impact then the tendency will for the club to release too early causing the ball to hook.

Remember the basics and only hold the club tight enough to keep control. You should not have any tension on your wrist and forearms. Practice the grip and check your results. Changing your grip should be slight, over compensating can cause other problems with your swing or begin to cause you to slice.

Most golf hooks are from a "strong grip", but in order for you to correct your hook properly; you must have the know-how and learn the basics of the golf swing.

Push

A push is a ball that goes directly to the right because of the action of the club. This should not be mistaken for a slice. A slice is an action of the ball spinning clockwise. A slice normally begins to the target and arcs away to the right, (left for lefties). A push is an action of the swing and is normally in an in-to-out swing motion. The opposite of the push is the pull, which is an out-to-in swing motion.

The push is caused by the swing path of the club. In the down swing, the path of the club will travel in an in-to-out path. Normally this is caused by throwing your arms ahead of your shoulders, being too close to the ball, and trying to over compensate your swing to make contact with the ball, or having your hips ahead of the impact area. These are the easiest to identify, but there could be other reasons.

The easiest way to fix a push is to go back to the basics of the golf

swing. The push is directly related to the action of the golf swing. Throwing your arms ahead of your shoulders, make sure that during your back swing, you push your arms out with your shoulders, and on the down swing, you pull your arms down with your shoulders.

At the point of impact you should be back to the same point as you were at your stance. Standing too close to the ball, check out your stance. The club face should be positioned center of the ball and the butt end of the club should be about 4-5 inches from the inside of the left thigh and in line with it.

Having your hips ahead of the impact area, again, you should remember to be exactly the same at the point of impact as you were at your stance. The push comes from an improper club swing and knowing the basics.

Shank

The shank is a missed hit ball off the club face. Other ways that a ball can be missed hit include topping, whiffing, blading, dubbed, or fat shot. All of these miss hits are the product of only a few things;

Not keeping your head down through your swing. Standing too close or too far from the ball.

Improper Club Grip.

Improper Swing Dynamics.

A shank is something that nobody wants to have happen to them. A shank is normally a product of not concentrating. Slow down, remember the basics, keep your head down, and concentrate on the shot at hand. The shank is one of the easiest fixable problems in golf.

Remember your training and get back to the basics. By getting back to the basics of golf, and learning the correct grip or proper stance, and using the proper swing technique will help in eliminating all of the problems with miss hitting the ball.

Those are the most common problems golfers find with their swing. There are also some very common mistakes that golfers make.

COMMON MISTAKES

It's difficult sometimes to hit a good golf shot. Some of us hack away at a ball hoping that we can get off a good shot and be proud at least for a few moments. But if we know what the most common mistakes are in the golf game, we can take steps to correct those mistakes and extend that pride throughout our game.

The Exaggerated Twist

Most people believe that the more they turn their backswing, the more distance they will gain. This is simply not true. Actually, to gain distance, you need to find the perfect posture and perform a fluid swing that will insure solid contact with the ball. If you exaggerate the twist, you will go out of the ideal swing plane and have to over-compensate to even make contact. Plus, the chances of coming out with a slice, a hook, or even topping the ball are much greater.

Rolling Hands

This is a common mistake and one that feels OK as you are doing it.

As the backswing progresses the club gets too far inside and behind you and the clubface is open, facing the sky. To finish the backswing you will lift the arms and put the club in a steep and weak position, maybe even getting it across the line.

If this is your mistake, you need to monitor how much the left wrist rotates early in the swing. Take the club back to waist high and allow only 90 degrees of rotation, so the back of your left wrist is parallel to your body line and the shaft is in line with your toes. The toe of the club should be almost vertical.

Disconnecting Arms

Many players begin the swing by pushing the hands out toward the ball and moving the left arm away from the body. As the handle moves out the club head moves inward, getting it inside and behind. The rest of the backswing is similar to the previous move.

The fix here is to keep your left arm connected to your left chest and moving across as the swing progresses. Visualize your hands tracking back with your body rotation, rather than moving out.

Picking the Club Up

If all you use to begin the takeaway are hands and arms, you will surely pick it up and chop it back down. The golf swing is a synchronized blend of club, hands, arms, and body movements, and they need to start together. If you are a picker, make sure the core begins to rotate as the club is put in motion by your hands and arms.

Club Head Starts Outside

The opposite of rolling the hands, this is often the result of trying for maximum extension or an overdone one-piece takeaway. Once your club is outside and above the plane, it must loop back under to get back on plane.

Lee Trevino perfected this move, and Jim Furyk is pretty good at it as well. But it is not something the average player can do consistently. Eliminate the exaggeration and work the club head back and up your plane line.

Standing Upright

Too many golfers stand too upright at address. Instead, their spine should be bent forward from the hip sockets until their arms hang freely. Players should also tilt their spine from 3-to-9 degrees on their trailside. This defines the starting move and helps you reach the 90-degree rotation needed for your upper trunk at the top of your backswing.

Two things derive from this trailside tilt: 1. it lowers your trail hand so that you can easily grip the club without stretching your trail arm or shortening your target arm. That way, you will not be inclined to move your trail shoulder, so that it points out towards your target; 2. It also puts your torso in a proper position to begin your swing.

A Bad Stance

The position you want to achieve at address is the well-known "railroad track" in which your feet, hips and shoulders form a line parallel to the target. That parallel line must be directed to the side of your actual target.

Most golfers do not achieve this setup and otherwise find themselves in poor address positions. That is because they step into the ball with their eyes on their feet or on the ball and the club. The end result is they mistakenly step toward the target, which forces them into a closed position at address.

Imagine when looking down the line of flight while stepping into your address position that your focus is keyed on a large tree left of the target. Now, draw an imaginary line from that tree back to your feet/hips/shoulders, so that they are parallel to your target line.

When hitting a short iron, align your feet/hips/shoulders directly to the tree. With middle irons, the alignment is a little to the side of the tree. For a driver, the alignment is farther to the side to allow for the optical illusion that makes your target appear smaller.

Here are some things to keep in mind when addressing the ball:

• Widen your stance when using a driver, so that the width measured from the center of your feet is equal to the outside of your shoulders. The width becomes proportionately less and less as the club gets shorter. That way, your ankles are under your shoulder joints.

• Close your stance a little, with your trail foot pulled back a little

more from the target line than your target foot. This is important, especially if you lack flexibility. You can do this with all clubs, even your wedge. It makes the rotation of the upper trunk to 90 degrees that much easier.

• The base of your sternum (center of your chest) should be pointing directly at the ball, so that your trail arm moves most effectively and stays below the target arm at the start of the swing and until it folds.

• Golf is a stability sport. Distribute your weight from the balls of your feet to your heels, but not to your toes.

• Golfers tend to stand with knees that are too straight. Be sure there is some flex in your knees, so you can use your joints properly. In essence, sit back with your hips out behind you in a skeletally balanced position.

Skulling or Topping the Ball

When you skull the ball, your club is coming over the top of it and you will end up hitting it “fat”. It won’t go very far, if at all, and you’re likely to be a little embarrassed at your mistake. Don’t worry; a lot of inexperienced golfers top the ball. There is a fix for it as well.

Put your weight in the middle, the golf handle left, weight on your left side, swing the arms up and swing the arms down in the downswing. Up/down makes the golf ball go up.

Hitting the ball fat is caused by the club being too vertical. If you go

too vertical, you'll wind up chopping the floor.

After you get all set up, make sure you're not leaning too far over on the left side. A little weight on your left side is alright, but the trick is to swing the golf club up on the inside. And that will give the golf club a little better angle into the back of the ball.

Be sure that you are looking at the ball and that you don’t rise up before you make contact. Standing up on the ball prior to the swing is the number one reason for skulling the ball.

Many beginners are eager to see where their ball is going after it is hit, but they look too soon and take their eyes off of the ball. This can also cause you to top the ball, so be sure to look at that little white ball until you hear it whooshing through the air. Then you can watch it land beautifully.

Chipping Problems

When you are chipping, a common problem that many golfers face is restricting your swing while chipping, not getting enough loft, or easing into the ball. To cure this, you should shorten the stroke instead of restricting your swing and don't ease into the ball.

Make a short backstroke and use a less lofted club if you feel the need restrict your backswing. Make a long follow through to allow for the necessary acceleration. Divots are not necessary, so hit down and through so you strike the ball with a slightly descending blow. You are likely playing the ball too far forward if you do not hear a click when chipping. The ball should be positioned just before the bottom part of your stroke.

Reaching out at the ball during address and impact, a player's arms

are almost at a 45-degree angle from the ground. It takes too much effort to hold your arms out at address and therefore it's even harder to get back to that position at impact.

To fix this problem, refer to the posture where the arms just hang in the natural position. If you feel like your hands are too close to the body then make the adjustment and kick out your rear end a little (check your weight distribution). The distance between your zipper and your grip should be around four knuckles.

Find a picture of a professional golfer and by using a straight edge notice how their eyes are over the shaft (approximately over the shaft label).You may have to bow more to get to that position.

Another big mistake is made when referring to ball position. Some players believe they need to change the position of the ball based on what club they are using. If the ball is played too far back in the stance, your shoulders will aim right and you will start the back swing from the inside and probably come over the top at impact (slice or pull). If the ball is too far forward, your shoulder will be aiming left and you will take the club more on the outside and loop under coming down resulting in a block or a hook.

To fix this problem, the ball position should be played one ball

forward of center for short to mid-irons, two balls left of center with long irons and fairway woods, three balls left of center with the driver. This may vary a little based on your swing arch.

Here’s a drill to help you with this problem. Take your swing with

the proper stance and posture and see where your club hits the ground. You should notice that it’s very close to the left center. If you are hitting the ground way before the ball, there’s a good chance you are not pivoting your hips or coming out of your stance.

So those are some of the more common mistakes made by golfers. Even if you’ve been golfing for years, you can still fall prey to these mistakes. Knowing how to fix them can be a great addition to your game and will eventually shave strokes off your score.

There are some shots in golf that will require some finesse in getting out of without amassing your score to new proportions. Let's look at a few trouble shots and get some advice on how to overcome them.

TROUBLE SHOTS

Because golf is such a complicated – yet easy – game, you may find yourself in some situations that seem impossible to get out of. We call these trouble shots. They can be frustrating and can add to your score in record proportions. Here are some trouble shots we've encountered and ways that you can approach them.

Deep Rough

Long grass has the effect of closing the face of the club and decreasing the loft of the club. For this reason, the player should use a more lofted club than if the ball were in the fairway. If a player has a long distance left, the first consideration should be getting the ball out of the rough. Use of lofted fairway woods #5, #6, #7 is advisable in this situation.

The long grass will decrease the loft of these clubs and the ball will actually go the distance of the less lofted fairway woods. Around the green, the player must again use a more lofted club. These types of shots are custom made for a wedge or a 9-iron. The effect of the long green will once again decrease the loft of the club. The ball will therefore fly lower and run more than if it were in the fairway. Remember; allow the loft of the club to lift the ball out of the rough!

Side hill, Downhill, and Uphill Lies

Nothing can be more frustrating than having a golf shot on a slanted surface. The way many golf courses are laid out, you will probably have to deal with a lie like this at some point in your game. But you can deal with hilly lies with no problems and a little advice.

Take a practice swing and note where the club is striking the ground. If the club is striking the ground nearer the back foot, move the ball back in your stance; if the club is striking the ground nearer the front foot, move the ball forward in your stance. This system is the most accurate system to determine where the ball should be placed in the stance. Seldom does a player have a purely side hill or uphill lie. This system takes all the factors into account as the practice swing is the forerunner to the actual shot.

The general rule of thumb is to position the ball in the stance nearer the higher foot on the downhill lies, and about center on the uphill lies. On side hill lies, position the ball left center (as you normally would). If the ball is above your feet on the side hill lie, you will normally hit the ball straight or pull it to the left. If the ball is below your feet, most players will actually pull the ball to the left because their leg action will slow down as they try to maintain their balance.

You will want to have a longer club than you would usually use for an uphill shot (a 4 instead of a 5). Choke down on the club and put more flex in your left knee (if you are right handed). Much of your weight should be on your front leg. Remember that the ball will generally go to the left, so aim to the right of the target. Position the ball slightly ahead of center and swing in a slow deliberate way maintaining your balance.

For downhill lies, you will want a shorter club than you would normally use (a 6 instead of a 5). The ball will go right, so aim to the left of the target. Position the ball so that it is back in your stance. Put most of your weight again on the forward foot. Have some flex in your right knee and then swing slowly and deliberately maintaining your balance.

Side hill shots are probably some of the worst in golf. If you are faced with a side hill shot where the ball is below your feet, you will need a longer club than you would usually use. Set up closer to the ball when you address it and increase the flex in both of your knees. The ball will go to the right, so aim left of the target and, again, maintain your balance with a slow, deliberate backswing.

When the ball is above your feet on a side hill shot, the stance is slightly different. You will still want a longer club than usual, but you will choke down on the shaft. Stand more upright and put more weight on your toes. The ball will go left, so aim right of the target and maintain a slow and deliberate backswing as you should be doing in all hill shots.

Restricted Back Swing

There are times when you will have a shot that will restrict your back swing. Let's say that your ball ends up next to a tree. You won't be able to take a normal back swing because the tree is in the way. You will have to make some modifications in order to get yourself out of this trouble shot. Luckily, it's not as difficult as you might think.

First position yourself so that you can get to the ball and still aim at your target. Practice a couple of backswings to see how far you can take the club back without bringing the tree into play. Then keep that distance first and foremost in your mind. You will need to cock your wrists and keep them cocked throughout whatever backswing you will be able to muster up.

Make a normal down swing, knowing that the club has room to miss the tree trunk and you will advance the ball into scoring position. The idea here is to just get away from the tree completely so you're not worrying about distance or even accuracy for that matter. All you want to do is get the ball back in the fairway so you can save your score.

Hitting Out of Water

The main rule of thumb when you have a ball in water is to just let it be and not try to hit out of it. However, if it truly is playable in shallow water, you may want to go ahead and try to hit it out and save yourself a stroke.

The key here is to play this ball like a buried sand lie with a nine iron which will not bounce off the water like a wedge will. Use a cut shot allowing the blade to slice through the water at an oblique angle and be sure to follow through on your swing.

In other words, you will want your backswing to be more outside of the normal line and then come back in across your line with the blade of the club open. Kccp your hands still in the swing as you won't want them to release and rotate. You may just find yourself back in the water if this happens.

Punch Shot

A punch shot is used when you need to navigate under tree limbs and other low-lying obstacles. You will use a punch shot when you need to keep the ball low but still get some distance on your swing. A punch shot is also used to get your ball out of trouble and into the fairway. So how do you execute a good punch shot?

You can use almost any iron to execute a punch shot, but generally, a lower lofted club will work best. Begin by choking down on the shaft and place the ball further back in your stance. Seventy percent of your weight should go mostly on your left foot if you are a right handed golfer – the opposite for you lefties.

Your backswing will be about ¾ of your regular backswing. Bring the club back making sure you keep your head down throughout almost the entire swing because making good contact in this situation is extremely important. Take the club back low and then finish low. What that means is that you won't have a normal follow-through as if you were hitting out of the fairway. But you do have to follow through.

The punch shot is easy to curve in one direction or another because you are generally using a lower lofted iron and they tend to exaggerate the angle of that loft. This shot is great for getting yourself out of a sticky situation involving natural hazards on the golf course.

The Flop Shot

A flop shot is a high shot that travels a short distance and is used to get over objects such as trees. It is designed to sail high and clear these objects easily. If you are unable to hit a punch shot and your only option on a hole is to navigate the tree, you will want to use a flop shot. It will sail high in the air and land softly on the green with little or no forward spin.

You can also use a flop shot if you have a pin that is tucked tight – or there isn't much green in between your ball and the pin. In this situation, you will need to get the ball up in the air quickly and land softly.

For a good flop shot, you will generally use a sand wedge or a lob wedge. The ball is played more forward in your stance and you will open the club face wide and choke down on the club. The club will be taken back using your wrists more than anything.

Cock your wrists quickly in the backswing and during the down

swing, you will release your wrists quickly. Your wrists will also cock in the follow-through. Essentially, this is a fast swing that requires you to abandon natural form to get the desired results.

Playing Into the Wind

Another of those trouble shots is dealing with the wind. Many players

advise teeing up the ball lower for a drive into the wind.

For average golfers it is better to tee the ball as normal and hit as solid a shot as you can make. The wind will exaggerate any side spin put on the ball at impact. This shot demands a solid hit with a nice even tempo.

Teeing the ball low will tend to produce a downward blow rather than a sweep through, thus producing more spin.

Another problem with the wind is club selection. If you find yourself a wedge distance from the green facing a headwind, try punching a 9 iron instead. Less loft means greater control. Stopping it will be no problem.

Our final chapter will be about a very important part of the golf game that many people just take for granted – stretching before your game.

STRETCHING FOR GOOD GOLF

The importance of stretching for your golf game cannot be stressed enough. Because a good golf swing requires that your body be in a relaxed, tension-free state, you will want to release some of that tension before you ever pick up a golf club.

The good news is that these stretching exercises are easy and only take a few minutes. That means you can effectively stretch right before you start your round.

For the first exercise, take your driver and place it across your shoulders. Stand with your feet shoulder width apart. Wrap your arms around the club at either end. Bend slightly back stretching your back muscles. Bend side to side so that you loosen up your side muscles and shoulders. Bend forward to extend your back.

Next, perform a partial squat with your golf club in hand. Stand with your feet shoulder width apart and place the club in front of you holding with both hands for balance. Lower your body by bending at the knees, not the hips, and raise the club at the same time. Raise back up and repeat ten times. During this whole stretch, you need to keep your upper body very erect.

This exercise will increase your blood flow and circulation throughout your body. This is a great total body warm up to allow your body to make a relaxed, comfortable first swing. It also increases the range of motion in your hip which encourages a more synchronized swing from the ground up.

Finally, you can do a standing rotation twist stretch. Hold a golf club chest high with the grip at shoulder width apart. While keeping your feet and hips fairly stable, rotate the club to the right and the left. Try to breathe out on every turn to release tension. Repeat each side ten times.

By doing this stretch, you will be preparing specific muscles of the trunk to make an aggressive move from the first tee on. This also prepares proper sequencing of the swing while warming muscles. This exercise will improve body movements during the swing from the beginning. This way you will not sacrifice strokes on the first couple of holes.

Conclusion: Final Words

We don't agree with Mark Twain that golf is a good walk wasted. It's a wonderful way to get out in the fresh air, enjoy nature, and have a little playful competition with your friends. You can get some great exercise on the golf course without straining your body which makes this sport ideal for any age group to participate in.

We do, however, agree that golf can be a very frustrating sport and one that requires a good mental state of mind as well as an attention to the body and how the golf swing works. It can be overwhelming – especially for the beginning golfer.

It is a great way to make new friends and business executives agree that the golf course is a wonderful place to make business deals and connections.

In order to make the golf game fun, you'll want to score well. With the tips we've offered you in this book, we think you'll be able to take strokes off your score when you employ the techniques we have outlined.

But nothing is quite as good for your golf game as practice. The more you play, the better you'll get. Practice on the course, practice on the driving range, practice in your backyard. Any time you can emulate swinging a club, you will start to learn about what will work and what won't when you get on the course.

Above all, don't be too hard on yourself when you get on the links. It's nearly impossible to perfect the game and you'll have your share of problems – it's almost guaranteed. That's why I think this quote can truly sum up the game of golf in the best way.

"Golf is so popular simply because it is the best game in the world at which to be bad"

CPSIA information can be obtained
at www.ICGtesting.com
Printed in the USA
BVHW041327060221
599513BV00008B/559

9 781801 570015